D1022127

<small>PRAISE FOR</small>

If You Want It Done Right, You Don't Have to Do it Yourself

"*The most common management style is seagull management. A manager gives you a task, disappears, and then only returns when you make a mistake—they fly in, make a lot of noise, dump on you, and then fly out. If you read Donna Genett's book on delegating, these ineffective flights will not be necessary.*"

—Ken Blanchard, coauthor,
    The One Minute Manager®

"*Delegating well brings a multitude of rewards. Genett gives us six easy steps to master an age-old problem.*"

—Patricia Crull, Chief Learning Officer,
    Toys 'R' Us; Chair, The American
    Society for Training and Development

"*Delightful, simple, effective.*"
—Jack Michaels, CEO, HON Industries

"*You can work hard, or you can work smart. Donna Genett shows you how to work smart.*"

—Gary Milgard, CEO, Milgard Manufacturing

"*This is the core skill of effective management and Donna Genett has written a wonderful book on how to become a better delegator—immediately!***"**

—Brian Tracy, author, *Turbo Strategy* and *Goals!*

"*This book took about an hour to read. By applying the simple, straightforward methods suggested by Donna Genett, I will earn that time investment back many times over.***"**

—Richard Hartman, Ph.D.
Product Development Director,
International Paper Company

"*This book not only teaches you how to delegate, it teaches you how to teach your boss how to delegate!***"**

—Paul L. Craig, Ph.D., ABPP,
American Psychological Association
Board of Directors

"*Genett provides us with six straightforward steps for creating ownership in the workplace—the best way to increase both job performance and loyalty.***"**

—Donald O. Clifton, Ph.D., Chairman,
Gallup International Research
and Education Center, coauthor *Now, Discover Your Strengths*

Effective delegation

- *increases job performance*

- *relieves job burnout*

- *boosts confidence*

- *reduces errors*

- *improves relationships among coworkers*

- *fosters competency*

- *provides a vehicle for mentoring and coaching*

- *decreases workloads*

- *builds teamwork*

- *elevates employee morale*

- *alleviates stress*

- *ensures successful results*

- *allows you and your staff to get more done on time*

- *is the key to reintroducing energy and passion into your job*

- *will change your life*

By implementing these six simple, immediately applicable steps of effective delegation, you will both prosper in your career and have increased time and energy for the off-hours activities you enjoy most.

If You Want It Done Right, You *Don't* Have to Do It Yourself!

If You Want It Done Right, You **Don't** Have to Do It Yourself!

The Power of Effective Delegation

by

Donna M. Genett, Ph.D.

Quill
Driver
Books

Fresno, California

Copyright © 2004 by Donna M. Genett. All rights reserved. No part of this book may be reproduced in any form or by any electronic or mechanical means including information storage and retrieval systems without permission in writing from the publisher, except by a reviewer, who may quote brief passages in a review.

Printed in the United States of America

Published by Quill Driver Books
an imprint of Linden Publishing
2006 S. Mary, Fresno, CA 93721
559-233-6633 • 1-800-345-4447 • FAX 559-233-6933
QuillDriverBooks.com
Info@QuillDriverBooks.com

Quill Driver Books titles may be purchased in quantity at special discounts for educational, fund-raising, training, business, or promotional use.
Please contact Special Markets, Quill Driver Books at the above address, toll-free at 1-800-345-4447, or by e-mail: Info@QuillDriverBooks.com

Quill Driver Books project cadre: Brigitte Phillips, Dave Marion, Joshua Blake Mettee, Pam McCully, Stephen Blake Mettee

10th Printing

ISBN 1-884956-32-7 • 978-1884956-32-4

To order another copy of this book, please call
1-800-345-4447

Library of Congress Cataloging-in-Publication Data

Genett, Donna M., 1955-
 If you want it done right, you don't have to do it yourself : the power of effective delegation / by Donna M. Genett.
  p. cm.
 ISBN 1-884956-32-7
 1. Delegation of authority. 2. Employee empowerment. I. Title.
HD50.G46 2003
658.4'02—dc21

2002156109

Contents

Acknowledgments 13

Introduction 15

° **1** °

Meet Jones and James:
So Alike, So Different 17

° **2** °

James Enrolls in Effective Delegation 101 25

° **3** °

Time for Step Two 41

° **4** °

James Defines Authority 51

° **5** °

Another Misstep but,
All's Well that Ends Well 67

° **6** °

Working with His Boss, James Applies the Steps
of Effective Delegation in a New Way 81

° **7** °

Why Is James Whistling? 87

About the Author 96

Acknowledgments

Thank you to my clients who have shared their hopes and fears, challenges and successes. It has been, and continues to be, a tremendous pleasure to work together. I have learned so much from you.

Thank you to my family and friends for their support and encouragement. Special thanks go to those who read the first drafts of this book and provided very helpful feedback and encouragement: Aleta Edwards, Michael Dennis, and Frank Hagel.

Thank you to Greg Winston and Warren Farrell for providing all the initial helpful tips about publishing.

A huge thank you to my editor, Joyce Quick, for her guidance and support, and for making the original work come alive. I hope this will be the beginning of many ventures together.

And finally, thank you to my publisher, Stephen Blake Mettee, for making the decision and the phone call that made this book a reality. I look forward to sharing this adventure.

Introduction

For the past fifteen years I have coached executives to achieve their peak potential. These managers came to me with diverse agendas and goals. The problems they (or their organizations) presented to me were as varied as their job titles. At some point in the coaching process, I inevitably came to teach each of them how to improve their delegation skills. Each student of this process was grateful, relieved, and eager to try it out. But the dramatic applicability and impact did not dawn on me until one week in March of 2002.

During this portentous week I coached twenty people. As usual, each client came to me with different concerns, from feeling overworked to wanting to learn how to develop his or her people to dealing with difficult employees. It seemed that regardless of their "symptom," the "cure" was the same: learning how to delegate more effectively.

I offer several consulting services so it is rare for me to have such a condensed experience in any one area as I did in this case. But the biggest eye-opener was to see how so many people consistently reacted to the delegation process I taught them. Comments like, "I wish I had learned this years ago!" "This will change my life!" and "Why don't they teach this stuff in graduate school!" were common. But the most frequent comment was, "Every manager I know could benefit from this. It's great stuff! You should write a book!" So I took their advice.

Having been in management myself, I knew I wanted to write a book that was a quick and informative read. One that gives you something you can do that will make a positive difference the minute you put it down. A book that is simple and practical, yet life-changing—if it's contents are put to use.

May you have the same reactions to this powerful process as my clients have had. Happy delegating!

◦ **1** ◦

Meet Jones and James:
So Alike, So Different

John Jones, Jr. and John James, Jr. weren't typical cousins. They grew up in the same town, on the same street, next door to each other. Their mothers were identical twins and best friends who married John Jones and John James at about the same time. Amazingly, the two men had also grown up as best friends. Even more amazing, the two John Juniors arrived on the same day, in the same hospital, with their mothers sharing a semiprivate room!

Because four Johns in such close proximity created confusion, the cousins were called Jones and James inside the family. In time, everyone else used these nicknames, too.

No one knew if the cousins' similarities were caused by identical-twin mothers. It didn't matter; the cousins looked and acted like twins. Before they were in kindergarten, they had discovered the art of deliberately confusing family and friends. In elementary school, they perfected it. In high school, they spent almost all their free time together, took the same classes, played the same sports. They were equally matched as both students and athletes.

The cousins attended the same college and continued to show up in the same classes. They took some flak about it, but anyone who was paying attention could see that they weren't doing these things out of some kind of dependence. The truth was they genuinely enjoyed the same things and got a kick out of doing them in tandem, so to speak.

After college, they continued the tradition of amazing everyone (at this point, no one was really surprised—just amused and curious) by marrying twin sisters in a double ceremony. They started families at the same time. They took jobs in the same company and mortgages on houses on the same block. What's more, they both did their jobs well. Everyone was happy. Things were looking good.

And, things *were* good, too, until Jones and James were both promoted into management. Their offices were on different floors, so they didn't see much of each other at first, and, for a while, each assumed the other was, as usual, duplicating his own experience. But that was no longer a safe assumption. James began to notice a difference. And it wasn't a little difference at that. Worse yet, it seemed to be growing!

You see, Jones consistently left home after a healthy breakfast and returned in time for dinner with his family. James's schedule was nowhere near so regular. In fact, James's Day-Timer looked like it had been in an explosion. He often skipped breakfast in order to get to the office a little bit earlier. When he got home depended on how many fires he had to put out that day and how deep things were piled in his in-box.

Not only that, Jones still did the things he loved; he played golf, made furniture, read books about the Civil War, took his kids camping. James, on the other hand, had so many things he *had* to do that he seldom had time for the ones he merely *wanted* to do.

For his birthday, Jones's wife gave him a Hawaiian vacation for two. James's wife was barely speaking to him, a fact that weighed heavily on his heart and mind.

Jones looked good—healthy and fit. Probably all that golf and sunshine. He still ran three or four times a week. When James looked down, he saw a pot belly, and he felt tired more than he liked to admit. The constant energy deficit had James hooked on coffee which he liked to think made him sharp but, in the quantities he was drinking, only made him edgy.

At work, Jones always seemed to be chatting and laughing with the people on his team, and he was involved in several company and community events. He clearly enjoyed mentoring others, giving his time freely. James didn't have any time to give. Besides, even if he could have found the spare time, he didn't have any spare energy. More and more, all he wanted was to finish the day and go home and crash.

James heard that Jones's boss was a happy camp director. He certainly seemed relaxed and cheerful around the troops. Matter of fact, everyone in Jones's department seemed relaxed and cheerful. No wonder. They were hitting and exceeding targets, cracking jokes, going home on time.

Sadly, James's department was getting farther and farther behind. They weren't meeting their goals. James's boss was worried and vigilant, James's employees were restless and grumbling, James's family was, well, restless and grumbling, too.

James hadn't been feeling too well either. Sometimes his neck hurt or his head ached, and he was beginning to feel hopeless about keeping up with Jones.

It didn't seem fair. Like his cousin, James had always been a top performer. When he had only himself to worry about on the job, he could do anything he set his mind to. Now that he was a manager, not only did he have to get his own work done, he also had to see that his people got theirs done. The work had to be kept up to company standards, too. If it wasn't, he had to deal with that. And, it was getting harder to get his people to cooperate. They didn't seem to know what to do. When they did, it took them too long.

The additional workload of a manager seemed tremendous. He had reports to write and other reports to evaluate. Memos and professional journals to read. Meetings to attend. On top of all this, he had to do administrative things—performance reviews, hiring, firing, and, more times than he liked to think about, disciplining.

James had gotten wind of several complaints, mostly about his never being available, but also some that he lost his temper too easily. But, with his workload such as it was, he had little time to spend out on the floor and he was often so tired and so stressed that he would forget to use tact.

His boss said he should delegate more, yet every

time James tried to pass some of his burden along to others, he ended up with more work to do, not less. The job wouldn't get done right, and it would fall to James to clean up the resulting mess.

James had always believed that, as his dad used to say, If you want it done right, you have to do it yourself. But now, he was reconsidering the wisdom of this cowboy-like self-reliance. What happens when you *can't* do it all yourself? When the job is so big it requires several, perhaps even many, people?

He had begun to wonder if the money that came with the promotion was worth the price he and his family were paying. Still, he didn't want to lose the income or the opportunity. He felt paralyzed.

In his car driving home late one night, after again missing dinner with his family because of problems at work, James came to a conclusion. He had to end his paralysis and do something. Something different. Perhaps even something he'd never done before. Perhaps several things.

Some of the different things might turn out to be difficult, others tedious. But that would be okay. He was tired of being tired and was willing to do whatever it took to get different results. The kind of results he saw when he looked at Jones.

By the time he pulled into his driveway, the question in James's mind about change was not when or whether, but how and what.

º **2** º

James Enrolls in
Effective Delegation 101

James had always been a pretty good problem solver, at least until lately. He figured the best place to start solving this particular problem was to talk to Jones.

For his part, Jones had been worried about James. He'd noticed how overworked and stressed James seemed for the last few months but he also knew his cousin well. In their families, unasked for advice was usually unwelcome. Neither cousin had ever liked giving it or receiving it.

Jones had decided he needed to stand back and wait for James to come to him. So, when James suggested they have lunch together, something James never seemed to have time for lately, Jones acted like it was no big deal.

But it was a big deal, in fact, it was monumental. For the first time, something very different was happening in their lives.

"So, Jonesy," James said, giving his cousin a playful punch on the shoulder, like they had done as boys. "How're you holding up? How do you like being a manager?"

Jones smiled. "I had my doubts at first, but it turns out I like it just fine. It seems to suit me and I feel I'm good at it. I like being more in charge. It's very rewarding."

James smiled back at him. Rewarding wouldn't be the word he'd choose. Time to take things a little deeper. "So, what, specifically, do you like about it?"

Jones tipped his chair back, rocking it a little. "That's a good question, and, as it happens, I've been giving it some thought lately. I guess one of the reasons is I like helping people grow and develop. You know, giving them a chance to shine. I like building a winning team and seeing how good it makes everybody feel. I like taking on new challenges and extending them to all of us, the whole team, and, well, kicking butt, so to speak."

Jones paused a moment and then continued. "Few things, in my experience, feel as good as being part of a winning team." He tipped forward again, onto all four legs, and looked at James, who was frowning.

"You don't seem to be overworked," James said. Jones nodded his agreement. James's frown deepened. "So, what's your secret? How do you manage? You have a clone somewhere who comes in a couple times a week while you sleep and does the work for you?"

Jones laughed. "Tell me where to get one! No, no clone, but my team and I pretty much share the workload evenly. It works out very well. I evaluate my team members' individual strengths and opportunities, and I consider their interests and personal goals, too. We talk about these things, one-on-one, and I try to divide up the work accordingly. I delegate." Jones wondered if he sounded preachy.

"That's too easy," James said, but his curiosity had been piqued. "It's like something out of a business school textbook. This is me. Tell the truth. When you give people work to do, don't they usually find a way to mess it up? Doesn't delegating just lead to more cleanup work for you, down the road a little?"

Jones chuckled. "Oh, yeah, that can happen, especially at first. I thought it was because my people were lazy or unmotivated or just not competent enough. Then Jennifer, one of my direct reports, set me straight."

Now James was keenly interested. "No kidding? How'd she do that? I mean, why did you need to be set straight, anyway?"

"Well, it's kind of funny now," Jones explained, "but at the time I was embarrassed. Taken aback, you could say."

"Come on, tell me," James said, punching Jones again. Just like old times.

"Okay," Jones said, warming to the task. "I forget exactly when this happened, but it was soon after I began managing the department. I gave Jennifer a small task to do. It seemed pretty straightforward to me and she seemed to understand what I was talking about when I told her to do it, so I went back to my office and waited to hear from her. Later that day, she came back with something totally different than I wanted. I wasn't happy and tried to tell her so, carefully, so I wouldn't hurt her feelings. Man, did I ever blow that!"

"What happened?" For some reason, it made James feel good to hear Jones say he screwed up. Jones is human, too, he thought. Good to remember.

"Right between the eyes. Man, she really let me have it!" Jones started to chuckle again.

"What? You're kidding! You let her get away with that?"

"Well, that's what's funny, in retrospect anyway. Everything she said to me was on target! She skewered me. What I thought had been her failure was really mine! And the conversation that I thought was going to be about chastising Jennifer ended up being about her setting me straight. Everything she said was right! I couldn't disagree. How's that for a humbling experience?"

James swallowed, cleared his throat. What was it that Jones found so amusing about being humbled, anyway? "So what'd she say, if you don't mind my asking?"

"Not a bit. All she said was the simple truth. She told me it wasn't her inability to do the task that was the problem. I knew she could do it, or I wouldn't have asked. The problem was my lack of specificity about what I wanted."

"What? Your lack of specificity? Run that by me again?"

"I asked her to do something she had never done before. I asked her to put together a flyer for our new campaign. I knew she was artistically inclined and thought she'd enjoy the chance to use her creativity. What she came back with was totally unlike what I had imagined and expected. It was out of character with our company image. Not only that, it didn't have the right content. She made a flyer, all right, which was exactly what I asked for, but it fell way short of the mark.

"When I started to talk to her about it, explaining all the things she hadn't done right, she kept interrupting: 'You didn't say it had to be that way,' 'You didn't explain it needed to be in that format,' 'You didn't tell me you wanted it to say that.' Finally, she held up her hand and said, 'If you had told me all this in the first place, I would have done what you asked and saved both of us a lot of time, not to mention this very unpleasant conversation!'

"Once I came out of shock, I realized she was right. I hadn't liked telling her she failed and she didn't like hearing it. What made it worse was knowing that she would have done a great job if I'd been clear about the specifics. We agreed that from then on we would both work to be certain she clearly understood my expectations. Now, when I delegate a task to Jennifer, I am explicit and detail-minded. I even ask her to repeat what I've said so I know she's heard me correctly. It's insurance."

James was silent for a moment, taking all this in. "Wow," he said finally, "it *is* simple, but it's really important. The truth is, I've never thought about it like that."

Jones smiled, punched James's arm. "Neither had I, old friend. Neither had I."

As James walked back to his office, he thought about various tasks he had recently assigned. He had made the same mistake in every case: He hadn't been nearly specific enough. Now he could see, from the perspective of his people, why they did what they did. Before this, all he could see was that they hadn't done what he wanted.

Inside his office, he wrote the following on his whiteboard, where he was in the habit of keeping many of his most important thoughts:

o *Clearly define and describe each task.*

o *Be specific.*

o *Ask for it to be repeated back to ensure he or she fully understands what is expected.*

That afternoon, James called Jason into his office. James had been thinking about a recent task he delegated to Jason. It hadn't gone well. The subsequent conversation about it hadn't gone well, either, and there had been tension between them ever since. For the past few hours, he'd been trying to see the situation through Jason's eyes, to see if what he had just learned could explain what had happened between them, maybe even improve things.

"Jason," James said. "Remember that job I assigned to you last week? The one we talked about later?"

Jason looked out the window. "Sure, I remember. How could I forget?"

Trying not to become annoyed, James continued, "Did you feel you really understood what I wanted when I gave the assignment to you? Please, be candid."

Jason looked at James, then out the window again. "Well, no, I guess not completely. But I thought I could probably figure it out. I didn't, as you explained already. Why do you want to know?"

James smiled, trying to put Jason at ease. "Well, I've been thinking about it, trying to understand what happened. So let me ask you another question. If you didn't fully understand what I wanted, why didn't you ask me to clarify?"

"Because," Jason said rather loudly, surprising both of them. He lowered the volume and continued, "I didn't want you to think I was ignorant or something. Besides, I was pretty sure I understood generally what you wanted. I just didn't realize about those specifics until you told me."

"I see." James rubbed his chin, which needed a shave. He really could see. From Jason's perspective, it must have been hard to ask for clarification. He was afraid of appearing less than sharp, so he assumed he understood enough to move forward. Of course, he hadn't. How could Jason know what James hadn't taken the time to explain?

"Thanks, Jason. That's all I need right now. I appreciate your help."

"No problem," Jason said, making his way to the door, still not sure what all this was about.

"One more thing, Jason," James added, sticking out his hand.

"Yeah?"

"I'm sorry."

Jason seemed stunned, but only for a beat. "Thanks, boss," he said quietly, as he shook James's hand.

James allowed himself a big grin after Jason had gone. He felt good for the first time in ages. He smiled as he walked out of the building and around back to the parking lot, saying goodnight to people as he went. He smiled when he got home, too, and everyone smiled back. They were happy to see James smiling again. It had been a long time.

The next day, James still felt pretty good. He worked on delegating more effectively. He sorted through the piles on his desk, making a small pile for each of his direct reports and a small pile for himself. He arranged each pile in order of difficulty. Then he chose one thing to delegate from each pile. He decided to start with the smallest, simplest tasks, partly because he knew he had as much to learn about the process of delegation as his people did about the things he'd be delegating.

He thought hard about each task before delegating it. If he were going to describe these tasks specifically, he was first going to have to be clear about them himself. What, exactly, did he expect? What should the end results look like?

Being prepared before he met with his people made him feel more confident. James went to his whiteboard and, above what he had written the day before, he wrote:

○ *Prepare beforehand.*

By 5:30 that afternoon, James had met with each of his direct reports. He explained clearly what he wanted each of them to do and what the results should be. He was clear about defining areas of the task that allowed for creativity or flexibility and clear about areas that needed to be done a certain way.

After he explained each task, he asked the employee to paraphrase back what he or she had heard. Sometimes, the person got it right the first time. Other times, minor points had to be clarified. He was painfully aware of how unclear he had been in the past, and he had a new appreciation for why his people kept letting him down. But still, he felt like smiling.

By the end of that week, everyone had completed his delegated task correctly. James was so excited and so appreciative that it showed. A great weight had been lifted from his shoulders. He felt cheerful, and so did his people. Everyone in his department smiled more that Friday than they had in a long time, including James. He felt proud of what they accomplished together.

When he got home that evening, his wife looked at him curiously. Something was different. James seemed relaxed, excited about the weekend. He had brought his briefcase home, as usual, but there wasn't much in it, and he was still smiling.

His family was skeptical about the permanence of this new good mood, but they liked it.

∘ 3 ∘

Time for Step Three

The following week didn't go as smoothly. On Monday, James took the next task from each pile and delegated it—in person. Since the easier tasks were out of the way, this was tougher to do than it had been the previous week and took James longer. After all, he had more to think about. He wanted to be clear in his own mind about exactly what he expected. He took more time with each employee to make sure the assignment was clear. Sometimes, he had to slightly change the way he explained things to accommodate a particular individual's style, but he didn't mind that. In fact, that part went pretty well. But, as the week progressed, a fundamental problem became obvious. People weren't getting their tasks done on time.

He wondered if they were resisting the extra work. If so, that could be a big problem, and James's team didn't need any more problems, especially since hope was on the horizon. It was time to take a breather. Time to talk to Jones.

"G'day, mate!" he said in his best attempt at an Australian accent as he walked into Jones's office and settled into a visitor's armchair.

"Ach!" Jones exclaimed, in a thick Scottish burr. "Gladdens me heart to see you again so soon, laddie. What's up?"

"Oh, not much. Actually been moving some work off my desk to my people this week. Feels pretty good."

Jones knew this was his cousin's way of acknowledging his help, showing that he used the ideas they talked about. "Capital! And how's it working out, old chap?" he said, trying for cockney.

James stood, walked over to the wall, and straightened a black-and-white photo of the Brooklyn Bridge. "Well, it started out okay. Actually, I thought it was going well. But now my people aren't getting things done on time." He glanced at Jones, who nodded and smiled.

"Ah, yes," Jones said.

"What do you mean, 'Ah, yes'? Has it happened to you, too? I thought you were square with Jennifer after that story. Happy office ever after."

Jones shook his head. "Uh-uh. Not hardly. That was just the beginning."

"Just the beginning? That doesn't sound good."

"Oh, but you see, it was! Not right away, though. No. I had a few more things to learn from Jennifer before I became an effective delegator. But, at first, things went pretty well. After our first talk, the one I told you about, I was pleased with her and with myself. That lasted a few days, until I gave the Simpson project to her."

"And what, pray tell, is the Simpson project?"

"Well, let's just say it was important and very time sensitive. I delegated it to Jen because I was sure she could handle it. I was clear about my expectations, what needed to be just so, what she had leeway with. I asked her to paraphrase what I had said back to me, and we both thought we were on track. By late the next day I hadn't heard from her, so I stopped by her desk and asked how it was coming. She told me in one word: 'Fine.' I felt reassured and basically said, 'Fine' back."

"Okay, so? What was the problem?" James couldn't figure out what he'd missed.

"There wasn't one, yet. Or, it didn't seem like it, anyway. After we repeated virtually the same scenario for two more days, I had had enough. I called Jennifer into my office, ready to be clear and firm. I even rehearsed what I would say. Made notes. You see, I was really disappointed. I told her so, too. I said, 'Jennifer, after all the work we've done to be clear when I delegate something to you, I can't believe you're letting me down like this.'"

James sat down again and studied the back of his

hand. "Okay...you told her. Of course, that was the right thing to do." He shot a look at Jones, then looked at his hand again. "Uh, you weren't angry, were you?"

Jones laughed. "Oh, no. Not me. But man, Jennifer was steamed! 'Letting you *down?*' she said, looking at me as if I had just poured blackberry juice on her new white carpet. 'Pray, enlighten me,' she said, 'and please be specific.'

"I have to admit, she had me a little worried at this point, but dealing with poor performers is part of a manager's job, right? So I came right out with it. I said I was sure she'd have finished the task in a day, two at most. I repeated that I was very disappointed. I reminded her that the project was time sensitive."

"Okay, so...."

"Well, at that point, she hauled off and gave me another blinding flash of the obvious. I have to tell you, it felt like getting hit with a water balloon. I remember her exact words. She said, 'As a matter of *fact,* I *didn't* know. You never *told* me it was time sensitive, and you *didn't* give me a due date or deadline. Were you expecting me to read your *mind?*'

"All I could say was, 'Ouch!' She had me again. *Her* so-called failure was really *my* failure to clearly communicate my expectations, and we both knew it."

James grimaced. "Man. So what'd you finally do?"

Jones shrugged. "Well, what could we do? We talked it over and added time frames to the list of what needs to be communicated when I delegate."

James nodded, smiled, got up, and gave Jones a couple of brotherly pats on the shoulder. "It's not exactly rocket science, is it?"

Jones shook his head. "Nope. But you do have to think about it. And, you do have to learn to build better rockets as you go along. We learn from our mistakes, right?"

Back in his office, James felt pleased that he was learning, not only from his own mistakes, but from Jones's, too. On his whiteboard, under the previous notations, he wrote:

○ Clearly outline the time frame within which the task must be completed.

James played a favorite CD on his computer and reviewed each task he had assigned that week. Several were time sensitive. These always caused the greatest concern and greatest stress. Yet, he had been so focused on making sure the guidelines for the tasks were clear and correct that he had overlooked talking to these people about timing! He had even overlooked *thinking* about it.

James established time frames for each task and talked again with each employee, clarifying deadlines. He was shocked that not one had realized time was of the essence. All were grateful for the clarification.

Once again, things seemed to be running smoothly in his department. James was smiling again. He dived into his own work, feeling confident that the tasks he had delegated would be done correctly and on time. He was again acutely aware that his workload had already shrunk, and he played with the implications for a few minutes. It felt good. Very good.

That night and for the rest of the week, James left the office an hour earlier than usual. At dinner

Friday, when his wife asked what had changed at work that allowed him to come home early, he got up and walked around to her side of the table, gave her a big hug, and said, "Me!"

James had the best weekend he'd had in months. Without that ever-present load of work waiting at the office weighing on his mind, he could relax. He actually felt lighter, and more lighthearted. On Saturday, he patched and sanded a beautiful old chest he had purchased years before at a garage sale. He showed his ten-year-old daughter the best way to sand wood satin-smooth. On Sunday afternoon, they had the Jones family over for a barbecue. It was the first Sunday in a long time that he didn't have to play catch-up to be ready for Monday.

"You know, you're looking good, James," Jones told him as he spooned out his third helping of potato salad. "It's been a while since I could say that."

James threw an olive up in the air, caught it in his mouth. "Thanks a lot, Jonesy," he grinned. "For everything."

∘ 4 ∘

James Defines Authority

James's department began the next week on a high note. Everyone seemed to be feeling good. James knew that the next task on each person's pile was going to be the most difficult so far, so again he did his homework before talking to each of them. As before, he clearly defined areas of flexibility as well as areas that must be handled a certain way. He specified the time frame within which the task must be completed, and spelled out deadlines.

He still felt a little impatient with the time it took to prepare. Part of him wanted to just plunge in and tackle the work himself, or simply hand it off to someone and hope for the best. But he knew where that road led. He remembered well the anxiety and frustration he felt before and he remembered what he told his daughter last weekend as they were sanding that old chest. "The more thorough the prep work, the faster it goes and the happier you'll be when it's done."

Once he had everything prepared to his satisfaction, James met with each of his people to share the newest tasks. He thought these conversations went well. Each employee repeated what he or she understood him to have said, and most seemed to have a good grasp on what they were being asked to accomplish. When there was doubt, James and the staff member discussed the project until both of them felt comfortable that everything was clear.

Each of his people seemed excited about these newest challenges. Did they see it as a vote of confidence, he wondered? Because, really, that's what it was.

James smiled as he remembered Jason stopping by his office earlier in the day purely to report that he was feeling more like the department really was "a team these days and I feel like I'm a contributing member." What great feedback! How often did stuff like *that* happen?

James's euphoria lasted until Wednesday's meeting with Josh, whose task was due. To his astonishment, Josh had gone beyond the bounds of what James wanted him to do. He had made a decision that had far-reaching impact. The result was embarrassment for their department, embarrassment in spades for Josh. For his part, James wasn't so much embarrassed as baffled. How could this have happened? He had been so careful. He spent plenty of time prepping Josh, who reiterated perfectly. He had been clear and specific. He had established a time frame complete with a deadline.

This time he detoured to Starbuck's for a couple of Americanos and scones before making his way to Jones's office. He wasn't embarrassed by a mistake made honestly by one of his people, and he sure wasn't going to be embarrassed by talking about it to Jones.

"I don't get it," he began before he even sat down, let alone opened the Starbuck's bag. "Tell me where I went wrong. I clearly outlined a task to Josh. I told him the time frame within which he had to have it done. He paraphrased back to me what I had said, and he had it right, okay? But Josh went way beyond the bounds of what I had assigned. He made a decision he didn't have the authority to make. Naturally, people have noticed, and they aren't happy about it."

"Oh, that," Jones said, peeking inside the Starbuck's bag.

"Don't give me 'Oh that,'" James sniffed. "I take it you don't think it's a big deal."

"Mistakes happen. In this case, no harm done, right? The word on the street is the company will probably survive. And, seriously, yes, the same thing happened to me. But mine was with...guess who?"

"Jennifer. You're kidding, right? You've sure had your troubles with her."

"Maybe, but you could just as easily say she's had her troubles with me!"

James bit off about half of his scone, nodded, and made "come on, tell" motions with his free hand.

"Well, as I delegated more to Jennifer, she continued to do great work and seemed motivated to keep expanding her responsibilities. It wasn't long before I gave her a sizeable project, more complex than those she'd handled before. When I explained it to her, I was aware that I needed to be clear about details and due dates. She seemed to understand everything I said. When she came to me with the result, I almost fell out of my chair! She had made commitments that she had no authority to make and involved people who shouldn't have been involved. It was a real mess."

James swallowed, wiped his mouth. "And, I have duly noted that the company survived. But what did you do? What did you say?"

"Well, you can bet I wasn't interested in a replay of our previous conversations, so I took a different approach. I asked Jen to repeat as much as she could remember about our conversation when I first delegated the project to her. She remembered well, so she certainly understood the task. Then I asked why she had made those unauthorized commitments and involved those people without checking with me. She said, based on what I had told her, that she had the distinct impression that this was her project from beginning to end and that she was to do whatever was necessary to make it happen. She said she felt making the commitments and involving the people she had were necessary.

"I disagreed, but what could I say? Once again, she was right. This time, I had failed to be clear about her level of authority in carrying out the assignment. Seems to me you made the same mistake, wouldn't you say?"

James was silent. Was this true? After all his work to make himself as clear as possible, had he failed in this important detail? For a moment, he felt uncomfortable, almost guilty, but it passed. He smiled broadly. "I *would* say. You're right, of course, Jonesy.

That's exactly what happened." A blush of relief washed over him. This was easy to fix. He was still on the right road; there had been a little scenic detour, that's all.

Once again, back in his office, he wrote on his whiteboard:

∘Define the level of
  authority along with
  the task.

But how do you define authority? Are there different levels, different kinds, James wondered. He thought about Josh and Jen and about other projects waiting to be delegated. Underneath the previous notation, he added:

1. The authority to <u>RECOMMEND</u>.

   Research options and propose the best alternative. Use this level when I want input before making a decision.

2. The authority to <u>INFORM</u> and <u>INITIATE</u>.

   Research and select the best course of action; inform me why it is best; initiate the selection. Use this level when I want someone to inform me before he or she takes action so I can intercept potential problems.

3. The authority to <u>ACT</u>.

   Full authority to act with respect to the task or project. Use this level when I am confident of someone's capabilities and the risks are minimal.

James imagined a grid to help him choose the right level of authority based on the task's importance, the project's inherent perils, and the knowledge and expertise of the person being delegated to. This is the grid he designed:

		Employee Knowledge and Expertise		
		High	*Medium*	*Low*
Importance of the Task and/or Project's Perils	*High*	Inform and Initiate	Recommend	Recommend
	Medium	Act	Inform and Initiate	Recommend
	Low	Act	Act	Inform and Initiate

That afternoon, James called Josh into his office. Josh seemed uneasy, prepared for the worst. He avoided eye contact.

"Josh..." James began. For a second, he thought he saw Josh flinch, but maybe not. "Sit down. Relax. I think I know what went wrong with that project I delegated to you."

"Uh huh. I screwed up," Josh said.

"No, actually, I think *I* screwed up."

Josh looked stunned. "*You?*"

"Hold on. I have a few questions first, to see if I'm on the right track. Tell me what you understood from our conversation when I assigned the project to you."

Josh remembered details even James had forgotten. "Okay, great. And what did you believe you should do in order to complete the project on time?"

"What do you mean? Whatever I had to, of course."

"Aha!" James exclaimed, bringing his palm down hard on his desk startling Josh. "Whatever it took! So, as far as you understood it, Josh, you were just doing your best to complete the project on time in accord with what we'd discussed, is that correct?"

"That's about it," Josh replied slowly. He was beginning to feel a little like he was in a courtroom. He didn't like courtrooms much. "So, sir, with all due respect, what's your point? I don't understand why you said *you* screwed up. I was the one who got us into hot water."

"Did you know you were getting us into hot water when you made the decisions you made?" James asked.

"Well, no. Of course not, or I never would have...."

James put a hand on the young man's shoulder. "Listen. When I gave you the project, I didn't define your authority. I didn't tell you how far you could go on your own. You did your best with the information you had. If I had been clearer, you would have come to me before making that decision and the water would never have gotten hot." He pointed to his whiteboard. "Take a look at this."

While Josh read what was written on the board, a slow smile spread across his face. "Okay, you sold me. I guess you *did* screw up."

James laughed. "That makes us even."

Josh laughed with him for a couple of seconds, then sobered. "I don't know if I said it, but I'm really sorry about the mess I made."

James nodded. "Thanks. Me, too. But now we know how to make sure it doesn't happen again."

That week was the best James had ever experienced since he'd had the new job. He left home at a reasonable time in the morning and came home to his family at a reasonable time in the evening. The piles of work on his desk were steadily diminishing, while morale in his department was improving. He had noticed people laughing and smiling more. They were contributing more, too, no question. As Jason said in his earnest, straightforward way, they were working as a team and liking it.

James certainly liked it. He had shorter but more frequent conversations with the people he worked with, and he enjoyed them more. The tension he had carried around in his body every day for so long he couldn't even remember when it began was now gone for long periods. Sometimes he dared hope it might never return.

Two things were certain. He wasn't holed up in his office all the time anymore, and his people seemed to appreciate that. And, he found that he liked giving out words of encouragement and praise and listening to people talk about how to solve problems and create better results.

At home, his family continued to notice changes. When James used to come home, he'd open a beer, hit the couch, and close his eyes. If a family member wanted his attention, the best time to catch him was at the table, assuming it was one of the rare days he made it home in time to eat with the family. After dinner, all he wanted was a newspaper or a little TV, then bed.

Now he spent time shooting hoops with his son and helping his daughter with her homework. All four of them went out for an occasional pizza, something they hadn't done in ages, and he and his wife often took a walk in the dark around the neighborhood before bed.

Ordinary things, but they felt so good! He wasn't a hamster on a wheel. He absolutely could keep up with Jones, if he chose to. And speaking of Jones, what a good guy. What a good teacher. What a good friend!

◦ 5 ◦

Another Misstep but,
All's Well that Ends Well

Two weeks later, as James was beginning to feel that he had it all figured out, another problem surfaced. This time, it was Jessica. He had delegated the last of the projects in the piles on his desk two weeks earlier. All were now due, including hers. They were the biggest, most complicated projects delegated so far.

When Jessica came in to report, she was beaming with pride. Her project involved many steps over a period of time, and she believed she had paid careful attention to all of them. But when James looked at the end result, he felt almost sick. He wanted to be enthusiastic, to not burst her bubble, but her results were so far off base he was stunned. Trying to buy himself time, James said, "Thanks for this, Jessica. I have something I need to take care of, so let me think about your project report. I'll get back to you as soon as I can." He needed to consult with Jones. Now.

As she left, Jessica couldn't help but let her body language show that she felt deflated. She comforted herself by noticing that James didn't seem angry. If he was, he didn't show it. He did seem disappointed, though. After all the hard work she had put into this project, disappointment wasn't what she expected and she didn't like what it portended.

On the way to Jones's office, James caught himself trying to figure out what he had done wrong this time. He was surprised by his attitude shift. Before, he would have been trying to figure out why the employee blew it. Now, he was asking himself whether he had once again failed to be clear.

"Big trouble this time," James said as he knocked and entered Jones's office. "Got a minute?"

"Sure. What's up?" Jones saved his work and swiveled away from the monitor.

"Well, I delegated this major project to Jessica two weeks ago. It was the last of the stack and the toughest one yet. I thought she was ready. I thought she could handle it. But what she came back with won't do. Not at all. Now we've lost two weeks on this thing, and that is not good. It'll have to be done over. And yours truly will be the one who has to do it."

"Hold on," Jones said, stretching out his palm. "There's no reason you have to take back the project. Your judgment of people is good. Always has been. Jessica can handle it. She probably just needs more guidance."

"From me? More guidance?"

"Yup. You're the man. Jennifer needed it, too, when I increased the size of her projects for the first time."

"Not Jennifer again!" James groaned and rolled his eyes.

"I can't help it," Jones laughed. "In some ways she taught me everything I know about delegation. If she hadn't been willing to take some risks with me, I might not have learned how to do it right. I'd still be working my fingers to the bone, digging myself into a deeper hole.

"Instead, this department meets and often exceeds its individual and team goals. My people are challenged and happy. This system of delegation provides a built-in process for developing people, coaching and mentoring them.

"And, since we have more successes, I have more reasons to recognize people's efforts, something I really enjoy.

"If need be, I even have clear documentation of poor performance, which, until you have to ask someone to shape up or leave, never seems that important.

"James, old salt, Jen made me a better manager. I owe her!"

"Yeah, I can see that," was all James could say for a moment. Then he remembered why he was there. "So, anyway, I must have missed something when I delegated this project to Jessica. I imagine you'll know exactly what it is, so enlighten me, cousin. I'm all ears."

"You're right, you did miss something. Just like I did with Jennifer. When a task or project becomes larger and more complex, it's important to build in checkpoints. They help you make sure things are going in the right direction.

"The checkpoints should be close together in the beginning of the project. Later, after the person demonstrates competence and shows he or she is headed down the right track, the checkpoints can be spaced further apart. That way, you don't let a lot of time go by during which the project is invisible to you. If things get off track, you can catch them before they get serious."

James nodded. "That makes sense. If I had done that, it would have saved Jessica a lot of time and energy. Not to mention...."

"...saving her butt! In fact, it would probably have ensured her success, don't you think?"

"That's true," James said, "and our conversation would have been much more rewarding than the short one we had, that's for sure."

"I think he's got it...by George, he has got it!" Jones kidded.

James grinned, but there was something he needed to know, and it had been eating at him. "Jonesy, why the heck didn't you just tell me all this right from the beginning? Why did you give me a little, let me mess up, then give me a little more? I have to tell you, you could have made it a lot easier for me."

"Really? Would it have been easier?" Jones asked, eyebrows raised. "Remember the first time you came in here to talk about the miseries of management? You weren't in a particularly receptive mood, as I recall."

James tried to remember. "That's probably true. Still, you could have told me everything then. I don't get it."

"Maybe I could have. Maybe I should have. But I figure sometimes it's better to start small and experience a few successes before moving on to something bigger. It's more internally convincing that way, know what I mean? Human Nature 101: We tend to be open to new and more difficult things if we've succeeded at some smaller, simpler things first."

"Just like with delegating. I see that. I forget sometimes, though."

"Yeah, I do, too. This has actually been a good reminder."

Both men were quiet for a few moments, thinking their separate thoughts. When Jones saw a smile begin to cross James's face, he said, "Uh, one more thing, buddy...."

"Yeah? What's that?"

"You're not done with the process of delegation yet."

"Don't tell me."

"Don't worry. There's just one more critical piece. I can tell you now because I know you're ready."

"You sure you aren't going to miss watching me fall on my face?"

Jones laughed, as expected. "Listen up. When the employee has completed whatever job you've delegated, always have a debriefing."

"A debriefing? That sounds like the Army. Be a little more specific."

"Well, I debrief on three things: what went well, what could be improved, and what we learned. I ask for an impression on each point, and I share mine. It shifts me from boss to coaching mode. I want to identify areas for growth, reinforce growth that has already happened, and applaud successes. Sometimes I need to use the debriefing to clearly outline areas of below-par performance, and clarify my expectations and suggestions for improvement."

"Man, sounds like a performance review to me. I hate those things, don't you?"

Jones laughed and shook his head. "Again, don't worry. This is actually one of the most valuable steps in the whole process. Long-term, even short-term, it makes your job easier and helps things run smoothly. Generally, it makes people feel good. It helps when it comes time for performance reviews, too. You make notes on everything, so it's all documented and dated."

James wasn't sure what to say. He stuck out his hand and said, "Jones, my friend through thick and thin, I want you to know that this means a lot to me. It sounds like a cliché, but this stuff is changing my life. My department. My family, too, I think. How can I thank you?"

Jones grasped James's extended hand, then pulled him in for a quick back-slapping hug. "Well, hey. A filet or two on the grill would probably work. Or some of those burgers with sweet onions you make."

"You got it. How about Friday? 6 P.M.? Bring everybody. We'll make it a party."

James nearly ran to his office so he could make whiteboard notes:

- ○ Set up checkpoint meetings to hear what's happening and to offer guidance, if necessary.

  (Set them up early and frequently at first, then taper off.)

He paused for a minute, trying to recall the last thing Jones had told him. "Oh yes!" he muttered to himself and wrote another note on his whiteboard:

○ *Conclude the delegation process with a debriefing session to discuss what went well, what could have been improved, and what has been learned.*

James took in all that he had written on the whiteboard, thinking about how these words had indeed, as he told Jones, changed his life. It felt amazing, yet it was really simple.

○ 6 ○

Working with His Boss, James Applies the Steps of Effective Delegation in a New Way

As James was contemplating what he had written on his whiteboard, he thought about other harried managers in the company who could benefit from this process. He started to wonder how he might share with them what Jones had shared with him.

While he was thinking about this, his phone rang. It was his boss, Jack, asking James to come to his office. This was seldom, if ever, a good thing.

"James!" Jack began as soon as James entered the office. "Don't sit, this won't take long. I don't know what's come over you the past month or so, but whatever it is, I like it. Keep it up! In fact, I'm so impressed with the changes in your department that I have a project I'd like to give you. A month ago, I wouldn't have been comfortable handing this off to you. Now I am."

"Well, thank you," James managed, not sure what to think or say. This was unexpected. He had been so busy working with his people on this effective delegation business that he hadn't thought about whether his boss would notice a change, or, if he did, what that might mean. "This is great. What's the project?"

Jack gave him a quick overview, then gathered up a stack of file folders and papers. "Here you go," he said.

A dozen, two dozen questions raced through James's mind. He wasn't at all sure he knew what was expected of him or how much time it would take. He wasn't sure about much of anything. Would asking these questions make him seem ill-equipped for this assignment? He stood there, holding the stack of papers, imagining that this must be just like what his people used to feel before he learned how to delegate. Could he possibly apply what he had learned upward, when *receiving* a project, as well as downward, when *delegating* one? He remembered Jones and Jennifer and decided to take the risk.

"Jack, I'd like to talk more about this project to make sure I understand what you're looking for," James said.

"Well, sure." Jack seemed a little surprised, but willing. "What do you want to know?"

James walked over to Jack's whiteboard and held up a marker. "Do you mind?"

"Not at all. Go for it." Jack was amused and he showed it.

"Okay. Here's what I'd like." James quickly wrote out a condensed version of the notes on his own whiteboard:

o *Desired results for this project*

o *Time frame for completion*

o *My level of authority*

o *Checkpoints for review*

They talked through each step, making sure Jack's expectations were clear to James. James listened, then paraphrased what he understood, each time asking, "Is that correct?" If it were so, they moved on. If not, they clarified.

James concluded by saying, "I think I've got it all now, so I'll get out of your hair. Thanks again, very much, for your confidence."

Jack put his arm across James's shoulders as they walked to the door. "Well, I want you to know I have even more confidence in you now. That was great work you just did."

All right! James knew he was going to succeed on this one. How could he fail? He finally understood what it meant to work smarter, not harder. If things kept going like this, he would be up for a raise soon, maybe another promotion.

That night he stopped at the supermarket and bought a big bunch of stargazer lilies for his wife.

"Wow!" she said when he handed her the bouquet and gave her a big hug. "Are you feeling guilty about something, or did you just find out about an inheritance?" She smiled at him.

"Nope, nothing to feel guilty about," James said, hanging up his jacket in the hall closet. "On the contrary, I just may have negotiated terrific terms for a new lease on life."

∘ 7 ∘

Why Is James Whistling?

On Friday afternoon, James was getting ready to leave the office for the weekend. He sat for a few minutes in solitude, reveling in the changes he'd experienced during the past few weeks. He had Jones to thank, and, as promised, he planned on doing so that evening with the best filet mignon he could find. It would be fun to get their families together for a celebration.

James looked around his office. He had a lot to celebrate. He could actually see the surface of his desk! The piles of paperwork were largely gone, some into file folders, some into file cabinets, some to other people's desks. He could hear some of his staff laughing outside his door. They were looking forward to the weekend, too.

His relationship with the others in his department had been transformed from one of avoidance to one of teamwork. James enjoyed coming to work again. His workdays were shorter, giving him more time with his wife and children. He was delighted with the time he spent with them, pleased that he didn't feel that he was neglecting his work to do so.

In truth, he felt like a different person, lighter, happier, more successful, and more fulfilled. He no longer felt the stress of constantly trying to juggle the different roles of his life. He had one life now, and it was definitely better. All this from learning the simple art of effective delegation. Who would have thought!

In front of him were the documents pertaining to the project his boss had given him. He knew he would really shine on this one. He approached his work with renewed enthusiasm and confidence.

James walked over to his whiteboard one more time. He picked up a bright blue marker. Whistling while he worked, he made a list of all the perks he'd gotten from becoming an effective delegator. There were even more than he had thought. Now that he had some spare time, maybe he could help others reap the benefits of effective delegation, too!

This is what James wrote:

Benefits of Being an Effective Delegator

o Gives me more time!

o Helps me focus on what's most important!

o Allows my people to grow in capability and confidence!

o Allows me to develop, coach, and mentor my people!

o Creates opportunities to provide recognition!

o Allows for clear documentation of poor performance!

o Ensures successful results!

Help others reap the benefits of effective delegation, share this book with a friend or coworker.

The Six Steps of Effective Delegation

o 1: Prepare beforehand.

o 2: Clearly define the task to be completed. Be specific. Ask the person to whom you are delegating to repeat the information back to you to ensure that he or she fully understands.

o 3: Clearly outline the time frame within which the delegated task must be completed.

o 4: Define the level of authority he or she is to use with this task:

Level one: The authority to <u>RECOMMEND</u>

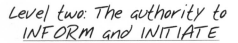

Level two: The authority to
  <u>INFORM</u> and <u>INITIATE</u>

Level three: The authority to
  <u>ACT</u>.

o 5: Identify checkpoints when
    you will meet with the
    delegatee to review progress
    and offer guidance, if
    needed. Schedule these
    meetings frequently at first,
    taper off as you see the task
    being mastered.

o 6: Hold a debriefing session to
    discuss what went well, what
    could have been improved, and
    what has been learned.

Donna M. Genett, Ph.D. is an author, international speaker, organization development consultant and president of GenCorp Consulting. With over two decades of combined consulting and senior management experience her information is highly relevant and immediately applicable. Her services of executive coaching, teamwork, organizational structuring, strategic planning and training are designed to maximize performance, productivity and profitability.

Dr. Genett's internationally acclaimed book, *If You Want It Done Right, You **Don't** Have to Do It Yourself! The Power of Effective Delegation* has been translated into sixteen languages. Her second book, *Help Your Kids Get It Done Right at Home and School: Building Responsibility and Self-Esteem in Children* is groundbreaking in its application of the management parable to parenting and helping busy professionals generalize their skills to the home front. Each book has clearly written workbooks and train-the-trainer materials to make learning and application easy.

Donna earned her doctorate from the University of Kansas. She grew up in Wisconsin and currently lives with her husband in California. She enjoys world travel, golf, skiing, home remodeling and sprint triathlons.

If You Want It DoneRight, You *Don't* Have to Do It Yourself!

Products & Services

Services

Speakers—Schedule a fun and powerful presentation of *If You Want It Done Right, You **Don't** Have to Do It Yourself!: The Power of Effective Delegation.* Great for large groups or events.

Workshops—Get the *Want It Done Right* training program delivered directly to your employees. This is an interactive workshop that takes participants deeper into the skills of effective delegation. **Available as a full day or half-day workshop at your location.** (Full day suggested for 40 or more participants. Includes one hardcover copy of *If You Want It Done Right, You **Don't** Have to Do It Yourself!* and one *Want It Done Right* Workbook for each participant.

***Want It Done Right* Webinar**—The exciting and powerful *Want It Done Right* Training Program is now offered in a webinar format. This format is perfect for small offices, or businesses with remote sites or a small training budget.

Train-the-Trainer—Your trainers learn everything they need to know to conduct an impactful training of *If You Want It Done Right, You **Don't** Have to Do It Yourself!: The Power of Effective Delegation* in your organization. Trainers will not only learn delegation skills themselves but will also learn to deliver a powerful training experience. This participative two-day certification includes all presenter materials as well as workshop materials to train 10 participants: one *Want It Done Right* Presenter's Guide; one *Want It Done Right* PowerPoint Presentation CD; 11 *Want It Done Right* Workbooks (10 for participants; one for trainer): 11 hardcover copies of *If You Want It Done Right, You **Don't** Have to Do It Yourself!*

Products

***Want It Done Right* Workbook**—This 36-page workbook, used in our training programs is great for individuals wanting to learn even more about delegation.

***Want It Done Right* Audio Book CD**—The powerful and effective training program of *If You Want It Done Right, You **Don't** Have to Do It Yourself!* in audio book format.

***Want It Done Right* Presenter's Kit**—The program to help people in organizations train their employees. Includes: one *Want It Done Right* PowerPoint Presentation on CD, one *Want It Done Right* Presenter's Guide; 11 hardcover copies of *If You Want It Done Right, You **Don't** Have to Do It Yourself!;* and 11 *Want It Done Right* Workbooks.

***Want It Done Right* Presenter's Guide**—The comprehensive guide for presenters to ensure a successful training program of *If You Want It Done Right, You **Don't** Have to Do It Yourself!*

***Want It Done Right* PowerPoint CD**—The PowerPoint Presentation of 75 slides used to conduct the *If You Want It Done Right, You **Don't** Have to Do It Yourself!* training. (Can be used as a slide show or to print overheads.)

For information about products and services, please visit
www.WantItDoneRight.com
Or call: (559) 875-7884

*Share the benefits of effective delegation
with a friend or coworker.*

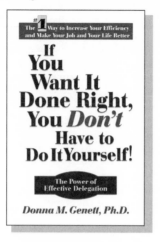

*To order individual copies of this book, please telephone
Quill Driver Books at 1-800-345-4447 or go to
www.QuillDriverBooks.com.*

*Please call Quill Driver Books Special Markets for details on
bulk quantity purchases for premiums, sales promotion,
employee training programs, fund-raisers or reselling at
1-800-345-4447 or e-mail
Info@QuillDriverBooks.com.*

---

*Did this book help you?
We'd love to hear how you
put this book to work for yourself
and/or your organization.
E-mail us at
Donna@WantItDoneRight.com.*